Meena and the Rabbit

Written by Jessica Ellis

Illustrated by Parwinder Singh

Collins

It is March.

Meena has a packet of seeds.

Meena puts the seeds in the soil.

Now she waits.

It rains and rains.

Meena sees a tail!

The sun is high.

Meena sees ears!

The rabbit looks for food.

Meena feeds it a carrot.

The rabbit seems better.

Meena feels good.

Meena feeds the rabbit

 After reading

Letters and Sounds: Phase 3

Word count: 53

Focus phonemes: /ai/ /ee/ /igh/ /oo/ /oo/ /ar/ /or/ /ow/ /oi/ /ear/ /er/

Common exception words: of, puts, the, she, and

Curriculum links: Understanding the world; Personal, social and emotional development

Early learning goals: Reading: read and understand simple sentences; use phonic knowledge to decode regular words and read them aloud accurately; read some common irregular words

Developing fluency

- Your child may enjoy hearing you read the book.
- Take turns to read a page, but encourage your child to read the speech bubble on page 9. Ask them to look out for sentences that end in exclamation marks so that they can read them in a surprised tone.

Phonic practice

- Focus on words with /ee/, /ai/, /oi/ and /ow/. Challenge your child to read these words:

  Meena   waits   soil   now

- Challenge your child to look for words with the "ee" spelling. (*Meena, seeds, sees, feeds, seems, feels*)

Extending vocabulary

- Read the text on page 12. Ask:
  - What seems better? (*the rabbit*)
  - Look at the picture. How can we tell the rabbit is feeling better? (e.g. *it's jumping in the air and holding on to the carrot.*)
- Look together at the pictures and support your child in making up sentences starting: Meena seems … (e.g. *Meena seems happy/excited*) Together, think of other sentences using the word **seems**. (e.g. *It seems to be getting warmer. There seems to be nothing good on TV. He seems happy.*)